IMPERIALISM

OUR NEW NATIONAL POLICY.

An Address
Delivered before the Monday Evening Club,
January 9, 1899.

By JAMES L. BLAIR.

This scarce antiquarian book is included in our special *Legacy Reprint Series*. In the interest of creating a more extensive selection of rare historical book reprints, we have chosen to reproduce this title even though it may possibly have occasional imperfections such as missing and blurred pages, missing text, poor pictures, markings, dark backgrounds and other reproduction issues beyond our control. Because this work is culturally important, we have made it available as a part of our commitment to protecting, preserving and promoting the world's literature. Thank you for your understanding.

IMPERIALISM

OUR NEW NATIONAL POLICY.

An Address delivered before the Monday Evening Club, January 9, 1899.

By JAMES L. BLAIR.

WHEN this subject was selected an "imperialist" was understood to be one who believed in a national policy looking to the addition of an unlimited amount of foreign territory to the national domain. Since then, it has been observed that "imperialism" means "the spirit of empire;" that empire connotes supreme sovereignty—greater even than that of a kingdom. Hence, the term has been repudiated by all those who are not yet prepared to go the full length of absolutism, and now those who are in favor of retaining the Philippines prefer to be known as "expansionists."

At this time it seems likely that we are to acquire these islands, and since expansionists, agreed on the main question, are divided as to the method by which such newly acquired territory is to be governed, the discussion so far seems to point to some such arbitrary form of rule as to indicate a future policy best described by the term first selected ; and hence it becomes material to consider whether or not such policy would be the part of wisdom.

The two principal reasons for the war with Spain were to free Cubans from the brutal inhumanity of Spain, and to enable them to set up a free government; the purpose to acquire further territory was expressly disclaimed. The President, on the 11th of April, 1898, said, in discussing the Cuban question: "I speak not of forcible annexation, for that cannot be thought of. That, by our code of morality, would be criminal aggression."

The active war with Spain ended in the signing of the protocol on the 12th of August, 1898; that instrument provided that Spanish sovereignty in Cuba should cease, that Puerto Rico and other Spanish islands in the West Indies, and an island in the Ladrones should be ceded to the United States; and that the United States should hold the City of Manila, pending the conclusion of a treaty to determine the disposition of the Philippines.

To the ordinary observer it would seem that with the evacuation of Cuba by the Spaniards the purpose of the war had been accomplished. But it was explained that Puerto Rico was to be taken in lieu of a war indemnity; that the island in the Ladrones was to be used as a coaling station and the question as to the future disposition of the Philippines was left open. When I say it was explained, I do not mean that the explanation came from the Administration. It is difficult to make explanations while you have your ear to the ground trying to find out what somebody else wants, so that explanations came from everybody except the Administration. When the treaty was signed on the 10th of December it was learned that, in consideration of $20,000,000, Spain was to cede the whole of the Philippine Archipelago to the United States.

The treaty is now before the Senate for ratification, without any explanation from the Administration other than its own terms. The logical connection between declaring war for the purpose of liberating an oppressed people in Cuba and the acquisition of an immense tropical territory to be added to the national domain at a distance of some 12,000 miles from our seat of government is not clear. It may be remarked, however, in passing, that the latest information at hand is to the effect that Agoncillo, the representative of the Philippine Government in Washington has asked to be recognized by the United States as such, and to be accorded the same rights as other diplomats; that Aguinaldo, the leader of the Philippine Insurgents has declined to surrender Iloilo and other strongholds, claiming them by right of conquest from Spain, and that Gen. Otis, in command of the United States troops, has been ordered to take possession of that city peaceably if he can, but forcibly if he must. This was ever the language of Austria to the Hungarian and Italian States; the kind of liberty which resulted from it to them is hardly desirable.

Contrasting this situation with the President's statement that "forcible annexation" would be "criminal aggression," suggests further reason for explanation.

The first question which arose in this controversy was as to the constitutional right of our government to acquire any foreign territory. Many able lawyers maintain that the government has no such power. The better opinion seems to be, however, that as a sovereign State it has. But even if we have not, there is no doubt that we may so amend our constitution as to acquire this power and so the argument is narrowed down to the question as to whether or not the proposed policy is a wise one.

At the outset of this question we are met by the assertion of those who believe in the expansion idea that it is no longer necessary to inquire whether we will or will not take this territory because the thing is already accomplished. It is ours, and it is simply a question as to what we are going to do with it. This proposition I deny, because under our constitution the President alone cannot complete a treaty; to become a law of the land the treaty must be ratified by the Senate. It is held by some that it is the duty of the Senate to ratify since to do otherwise would discredit our national representatives at Paris and the Administration. This view seems to me to be begging the question, and if it is the correct one, then we should discard our constitutional fiction and by amendment lodge the power of making treaties solely with the President. No harm could come from a rejection of the treaty for stated reasons. Whereupon the President could re-open negotiations and modify its terms in accordance with the will of the people as expressed through their representatives. The view that the President alone should have the treaty-making power would transfer the law-making functions of Congress to the Executive.

The arguments in favor of expansion are substantially as follows:

We need more territory for our national development;

England has demonstrated that a colonial policy is a wise one;

That this particular territory is specially desirable;

That its acquisition will extend our commerce and enrich our people:

That by taking this territory we shall get rid of our policy of isolation and take our place at the council board of the nations of the earth ;

That we shall be in better position to prevent the dismemberment of China ;

That the flag has been raised at Manila and where the flag has once been raised it must never be pulled down ;

And that since we have overthrown Spanish government in Manila a moral obligation rests upon us to retain the whole property so as to maintain order and prevent anarchy.

Let us examine these reasons in their order.

The total area of the United States and Alaska is 3,501,000 square miles.

The public domain at present is about 9,000,000 acres, and in addition to the public lands there are vast areas owned by individuals available for settlement at nominal prices. The ratio of population to territory is one person to every thirty acres or about twenty to each square mile. The entire population of Europe could be set down in the Mississippi Valley without producing a congestion of population. It is not apparent, therefore, that we need at the present moment to annex a million and a half acres situated in the China Sea, on this score. Would it not be better to buy, if we need it, contiguous territory from Mexico or Canada?

The colonial policy of England was a necessity. Her congested population, her great surplus product of manufactured goods, the importance of finding opportunities for investment for the great wealth of her people, are among the reasons why this is so. That policy in the beginning was accompanied by acute abuses and it is not as is so often asserted, the reason of her commercial supremacy, which is wholly due to the cheapness and merit of her manufacturers. The notion that trade follows the flag is an exploded one. Trade follows the price list ; and in the case of England the flag has followed her trade. Her merchants have penetrated to every part of the earth and her wars and acquisition of territory have followed upon the heels of attacks made upon her citizens trading in foreign lands. The notion that a nation must be conquered by force of arms in order that its trade may be secured is one of the oldest of fallacies. Moreover, the fact that Canada maintains a protective tariff duty against English goods and that Australia now purchases more goods from Germany than she does from England, would seem to indicate that the ownership of colonies does not insure the retention of their trade. It is well known that England's colonies cost her more than their revenues; her colonial budgets have been the plague of her statesmen for generations; and Macaulay says that "Colonial Empire has been one of the greatest curses of modern Europe; and that its results have been "wars of frequent occurrence and immense cost; fettered trade; lavish expenditure, clashing jurisdiction, corruption in government and indigence among the people."

The Philippine Archipelago contains about 200 Islands of substantial size and in all about 1400, many of which are mere volcanic rock points jutting above the surface of the sea. There has never been a reliable census but its population is estimated at between 8,000,000 and 10,000,000 composed of about 5000 Europeans and the remainder of Malays, Chinese, Moslems and other savage and semi-civilized people.

Let us see what its commercial advantages are likely to be. In the ten years ending 1897 there were annually exported hemp and sugar to the value of about $9,000,000, of which more than fifty per cent. came to this country. These are the only exports of any considerable value and of all the rest we had all we wanted. We could have had and we can have in the future every article exported if we are willing to pay for it. It is hard to see, therefore, how ownership will help matters unless we intend to force them to sell us their products at our own prices, just as we are making Spain sell us the islands at our valuation of $20,000,000.

But it is said we will sell them more goods. It goes without saying we could have sold them everything they consumed, except what Spain compelled them to buy, if we sold cheap enough. We sell to the colonies of every other nation, in spite of protective tariffs, because we produce many of the cheapest and best articles of commerce. No artificial restrictions will long withstand the power of cheap and good manufactures. We can only improve on the present situation by coercing our new colonists into taking more goods at our own prices.

At the beginning of this question we must remember that we are pledged to maintain what is technically known as the "open door" in these islands. That is to say, we cannot, under the treaty, exclude Spain from trading with the Philippines for ten years, and, as many maintain, we are under obligation to permit England to enjoy the same advantages as ourselves, since our success in the

Spanish war is largely due to the fact that Great Britain gave early notice that any interference with our operations by European Powers would be taken by England as a *casus belli*. So far as can be ascertained Spain has enjoyed a monopoly of all imports to the Philippine Islands wherever she could furnish them. Notwithstanding this fact, we have exported to the Philippines a fair amount of all shipments made to that country for the last ten years. For the next ten years at least Spain will have the same opportunity which she has heretofore had, and similiar privileges must be accorded to England for all time. How, then, is our attitude improved by annexation, unless (and this, indeed, is the only way in which the opening up of this new market can benefit us) the consumption of the Filipinos is greatly increased. Friends of annexation assert that this will be the result. That the introduction of American methods, machinery and colonists to these islands will so develop their natural resources as to greatly increase the food and manufactured products consumed by the inhabitants. Here we enter into a purely speculative field, with nothing to instruct us except the fact that it is one of the immutable laws of nature, abundantly sustained by history, that the inhabitants of the temperate zone never will colonize in the tropics in sufficiently large numbers to change the character of population. Climate, disease, and other considerations are the natural barriers which exclude from such lands practically all intelligent Europeans. Colonists are restricted to those who go as managers of plantations or factories, and for the purpose of exploiting the resources of such countries. Necessarily, the number of such is limited, and the result has always been, and must always be, that in these islands there will be a thin sprinkling of Europeans, employing and directing native labor. That this will increase production and therefore consumption goes without saying, but to what extent it is impossible to assert. Individuals and corporations will of course profit by this occupation, but the statement that any considerable number of our people will transfer their residences to these islands need only to be made to refute itself. It is contrary to the teachings of history and to the dictates of self-interest. This much, however, is certain : That in pursuance of fixed economic laws, whoever is able to furnish most cheaply those articles which are most desired, will always be able to take the market from the dearer producer. The fact is well established that our own labor, which is the highest paid in the world, is the cheapest, because of its extraordinary skill and capacity for production. We are already underselling England in many of her own colonies. We have long supplied many of the most important articles of commerce to these, as well as to Spain's other colonies, and we are therefore bound to conclude that the only additional commercial advantage which will come to us from the ownership of the Philippines will be that nebulous, undemonstrable increment of consumption which will be created by the injection into that country of American enterprise and intelligence. That our whole people will be thereby enriched is an open question. The burden of proof is upon the expansionist. That some will be enriched is unquestioned, but the number will probably be limited to those upon whom the Secretary of War confers the special privileges which he is now giving to enterprising American syndicates in Cuba and Puerto Rico.

Our policy of isolation, as it is called, probably originated in that wise, and as it now seems, pathetic, appeal of Washington in his Farewell Address. We are now told by certain wise men that our nation has become a giant, and "is no longer content with the nursery rhymes which were sung around its cradle;" that it has outgrown "the swaddling clothes" made by Washington and Madison. Let us for a moment, in the spirit of reverence which the utterances of that great man have always heretofore inspired, read again one of those "nursery rhymes" from the Farewell Address: "Why forego the advantages of so peculiar a situation?" (that is, isolation.) "Why quit our own to stand upon foreign ground? Why, by weaving our destiny with that of any part of Europe, entangle our peace and prosperity in the toils of European ambition, rivalship, interest, humor, or caprice?" If these be not words of wisdom, or if, adopting the metaphor of the wise men of to-day, these be not garments in which any brave self-respecting and prudent "giant" may clothe himself; if they be not the utterances of patriotic statesmanship, conforming to the approved precepts of political economy, may we not ask wherein have we so changed, what are the new conditions which have made foolish the wisdom of our forefathers? This policy has conduced as much perhaps as any other policy of this nation to its aggrandizement. It was the parent of the wise and timely utterance of President Monroe which has kept this country free from the encroachments of monarchy, and reserved as a haven (isolated, it is true, but isolated only from that which was effete and evil in the old world) for the growth of liberty and progress. "Taking a seat at the Council Board of Nations" is an attractive, but it is submitted rather a misleading phrase. If it be analyzed it can mean nothing more nor less than that we shall take part in that unending war of diplomacy in which European nations have been for centuries engaged, and which is still their chief employment. It means that when the Turk oppresses the Armenian, we shall be called upon to take part in the affair, and forced perhaps into an unjust and bloody war. It means that when the aggressive Russian demands his slice of Chinese territory, we shall be obliged to ally ourselves with other European powers to say, "Thus far and no farther." It means that we shall thrust ourselves into these very entanglements with foreign nations against which that wise and great, but out of date, statesman the father and founder of our Republic, warned us. In a word it means that we shall enter at once, and without preparation, into that dangerous, though dazzling contest with trained diplomatists upon the chess-board of Asia and Africa, for prizes which we neither need nor want, and with no reward but the empty satisfaction of having helped to preserve that precarious, evanescent entity, the "balance of power" in Europe. It is to our glory that our diplomats have not in the past been trained specialists. It was unnecessary that they should be so, because we had shunned these perilous entanglements which in the "nursery rhymes" of the fathers we were counseled to avoid, whereby we escaped the bloody wars, the hideous social revolutions, the spectre of anarchy, and the internecine strife which has tyrannized the civilization of Europe for hundreds of years. This so-called policy of isolation, then, which affords that safety naturally proceeding from the fact that we were separated by natural barriers from other nations and the dignity arising from the fact that we are a self-respecting, just people who observe that first law of intercourse, namely, attend strictly to our own business; this policy of isolation, then, is good to abandon; and why? In order that we may become a "world power." In order that we may take part in the never ending strife for more territory. In order that we may preserve an equilibrium amongst the armed camps of Europe. In order that we may help or hinder the national greed for territory, the avarice of empire which dominate the policies of European nations — into which they are driven as the only outlet for the turbulent discontent of their people. May we not in all soberness ask: Is this the destiny, which some have called the duty, of a free people?

The Philippines are distant about 700 miles from the nearest point in the Chinese Empire. Events seem to point to the fact that Great Britain, Russia, Germany and France are maneuvering for the partition of the Flowery Kingdom. Whether or not this be so need not concern the people of the United States unless, forsooth, we have already taken our seat at the "Council Board of Nations." If it be so, the fact that we have possessions in the China Sea, that we shall have in the harbor of Manila a squadron (assuming that we send there our entire navy) about one-seventh the size of Great Britain, about one-fifth that of France, about one-third that of Russia and about one-half that of Germany or Japan, and that we send thither our entire army, ranking in point of number in the relation of from one-fourth to one-half as large as those of these several Powers, what earthly influence can we be expected to exert upon the situation? Every nation of Europe would unite against us on the main proposition of the partition of China and our sole influence would consist in the formation of combinations with one or the other for the purpose of fixing the share of each. Relative to the whole our armament, independent of efficiency, is so ridiculously small that it is scarcely worthy of discussion. And whatever our moral influence might be, would it not be absolutely destroyed by the fact that we shall be protesting against the partition of one country when we have recently forced a conquered nation to yield to us its territory at a price wholly inadequate? Do we not stultify ourselves when with our hands yet red with the forcible conquest of the Philippines, we say to Europe "you shall not dismember and partition the Chinese Empire?"

Sentiment has always been a potent factor in the making of history. The map of Europe has more than once been changed by it. There is no higher sentiment on earth than that which glorifies the national flag, because it is a sentiment rooted in patriotism, of which the least that can be said is that it is the national religion. But the dividing line between sentiment and sentimentality, the weakest and silliest of motives, is often very narrow. The sentiment which glorifies the emblem of freedom is noble and exalted. The sentimentality which concedes the claims of rank and birth and admits the divine rights of kings is puerile and absurd. The sentiment which hedges about the chief magistrate chosen by a free people with the dignity and respect of his great office is manly and patriotic. The sentimentality which subjects a people to the licentious tyranny of a George IV is beneath contempt. The American flag is but red, white and blue bunting, but it symbolizes the genius and the aspirations of a great and free people. When it has once been raised in the cause of freedom and justice the hand that pulls it down until that cause is won, is the hand of a traitor. But when once it has been raised by an unauthorized hand or in a cause which the sober sense of the people has determined to be wrong, when, in a word, it ceases to be the emblem of freedom and equal rights to all, then the hand which fails to pull it down is the hand of a man who is recreant to his nation's honor. It was once unfurled on Canadian soil and in Tropoli; it once waved on the heights of Chapultepec and Monterey. In each case it was unfurled by the hands of men as patriotic as any who now live, but the greed of conquest had not then seized upon our people; and when the fight was won, the treaties signed, the nation's honesty and honor vindicated, that same flag was pulled down by the same hands that raised it, with no thought of infidelity, because it was in the course of duty. Let us not be misled by a phrase, let us not mistake shibboleth for a Marsellaise. Let us remember that the words of the "Star Spangled Banner" are, "Long may it wave, o'er the land of the free and the home of the brave." To raise that flag over a huddle of barbarians, admittedly unfit for citizenship, for the purpose of holding them indefinitely under a military dictatorship, may be simply a mistake, but such a mistake persisted in may become a prostitution of that national emblem to the perpetration of a national crime; the calm judgment of our people may render the verdict that the traitor's hand is not his who pulls it down, but his who keeps it flying for the perpetuation of a great wrong.

The argument that by the taking of Manila we incurred a moral responsibility to occupy and civilize the inhabitants of these islands, seems inconclusive because based upon the tenuous assumption that anarchy would follow our withdrawal. Our navy happened to find a Spanish fleet in Manila harbor and destroyed it. Subsequently the army captured and held the City of Manila. Our government carefully avoided any alliance with Aguinaldo and his services rendered Dewey were wholly voluntary. This was a mere incident of the war. We could at any time have withdrawn from Manila, restoring the property to Spain. We are no more obliged to remain there because the condition of the natives is said to be bad than we are to go to the Carolines or to Spain itself. The condition of the lower classes in Spain is in many respects quite as bad as was that of the Cubans. The declared purpose of the war was to relieve the Cubans ; that is accomplished. We must stop at that point or we must recognize the logic of the situation. If we are bound to relieve the Filipinos we are bound to relieve the oppressed subjects of Spain wherever we find them and we are bound by the same token to go in search of them. If it be said it would be barbarous to leave them under the tyranny of Spain, the answer is, it is quite as barbarous to leave the inhabitants of the Caroline Islands under her tyrannical heel. We could have exacted from Spain in the treaty guarantees of proper treatment of the Filipinos, or we could, with equal propriety have announced to the other civilized powers of the earth that by an accident of the war we had come into possession of a property which we could not in honor keep and which we felt we ought not to restore to Spain. A protectorate over the Philippines could have been established just such as the European Powers are maintaining over Crete. The danger of a partition of this territory is no greater than in the case of Crete or any other weak government. If wars should result they need not be upon our national conscience. We should have done the right thing and are not responsible for the consequences.

Thus it would seem that we do not need more territory as such; that the wisdom of the colonial policy of England is not demonstrated; that this particular territory is not especially desirable; that its acquisition will not enrich our people and extend our commerce; that taking our place at the "Council Board of Nations" is not in itself the greatest good; that we can scarcely prevent the dismemberment of China; that the moral responsibility argument is subtile and obscure, and that it is not decisive of the whole question to wrap ourselves in the national flag and have a fit. In addition to these considerations may be added the following :

It is a fact well established by history that not one tropical district on the face of the earth is occupied exclusively or by a majority of people of northern stock. There are many of such stock residing in the tropics, but only temporarily and for the specific purpose of gain, and hence their influence upon the social and economic conditions of the servient race is usually for evil. There is no tyranny like the tyranny of a highly civilized race over a degraded one. The inevitable result of the acquisition of the Philippines, socially considered, would be the domination of an oligarchy of whites over a heterogeneous mass of uncivilized natives. Such a condition infallibly brings into play that quality of human nature which always crops out whenever opportunity arises, expressed in the statement that "nine-tenths of mankind were born bridled and saddled with the other tenth booted and spurred to ride them," and which results in the deterioration of both oppressor and oppressed.

More than three hundred years of Spanish occupation have demonstrated this fact in this particular locality. The same is true of Jamaica, Batavia, Borneo and Sumatra. The social condition of the natives has not been appreciably raised. That of such few Europeans as have permanently resided there has been appreciably lowered, since the effect of a tropical climate upon the physical and intellectual energy of Europeans is well known to be permanently injurious.

The population of these islands number somewhere from eight to ten millions, from one-tenth to one-eighth of our own population. Its composition includes the following: Pure Malays, Spanish Malay, half-breeds, Chinese half-breeds, Chinese Coolies, Spanish Creoles, and a few Europeans (including Friars), who in 1845 numbered about 4000 and whose number can not now be definitely ascertained. There are about one hundred thousand Malays who are Moslems and from thirty to forty thousand Negritos or pure unadulterated savages. More than forty different languages are spoken in the islands and many of the tribes have never been subjugated by Spain. The City of Manila and its surroundings contains about three hundred thousand people of whom not more than ten per cent. are foreigners (other than Chinese), the remainder being made up of native Malays, half-breeds of all kinds, Spanish and Chinese. The Malay is described by one who has lived many years in the colonies as a gambler, a profligate, indolent, untruthful, even in the confessional, disobedient, cruel to animals and enemies, and superstitious. These number considerably more than half of the entire population. The Moslem population is warlike, fanatical and dangerous. They compose the bulk of the piratical bands which are to be found all along the coasts of these islands and some of them within half a day's journey of Manila.

The Negritos, or Aetas, are black savages, closely resembling Apes in shape and tree climbing habits, dwelling in mountains and forests, clothed only in girdles; they are believed by those who know them best to have cannibalistic habits, and are worshippers of the moon. A high authority is of the opinion that nothing short of actual imprisonment will ever subjugate either these blacks or the Malay population. The actual control of Spain has never extended beyond a day's journey from the great cities on any of the principal islands. So far as the quality of their population is concerned it can scarcely be considered as desirable except as affording opportunities for missionary work; but it would hardly seem to be necessary to conquer them in order to evangelize them. The result of the efforts of the Roman Church in this direction for some 350 years does not seem to be a shining success. Now whether we are to take these people in as citizens or subjects is one of the questions which is to be solved. If as citizens, they would seem as yet hardly qualified for self-government. If as subjects, they would, of course, be more manageable; but whatever we decide to do with them we must not forget that the fourteenth amendment of the Constitution provides that: "All persons born or naturalized in the United States, or subject to the jurisdiction thereof, are citizens of the United States," and the fifteenth amendment enacts that: "The rights of citizens of the United States to vote shall not be denied or abridged by the United States or by any State on account of race, color or previous condition of servitude." It is maintained by some that these provisions apply only to person in States and not in territory other than States, but even if the opposite be the true construction it follows that unless permanently held in subjection by military power these people will one day be entitled to vote, and we may meet with even greater perplexities than those which forced the government to disfranchise all persons in the District of Columbia, in order to suppress the negro vote.

One of the problems which we must solve will be as to the method of government to be adopted. We are committed by the Act of Congress to the proposition that all of the people of Cuba "are and of right ought to be free" and that they must be given an opportunity to form a free government. We must assume the same to be true as to the Filipinos. The administration, however, has not seen fit to suggest any particular method and we are therefore left to speculate as to which will be selected.

There have been in history various forms of colonial government. First, that of the Chartered Company adopted by England in India, which resulted in that case in such appalling corruption that it was superseded by the present system of civil administration headed by the Viceroy of the Crown and supported by a military establishment of about 75,000 men. The Chartered Company method was, of course, and would always be, barbarous and tyrannical in the extreme. The Warren Hastings which it produced in India would dwindle into insignificance beside the Tweeds and the Crokers which this new political Golconda would develop. The civil system of India is the growth of nearly a century, and is the result of the fact that the English take the business of governing seriously and give their best men and efforts to it. We are utterly unequipped with any such system. Our best men are not attracted to the public service and those who offer are chiefly political placemen. We have no right to expect from the present administration any better appointments, if such a system is adopted, than those made during the recent war which were dictated by political influence, under a suspension of the civil service reform law and were productive of infinite expense, mal-administration, suffering and death. The civil service of India is well nigh perfect; that of this country is still in the midst of its mortal struggle against the spoilsman. The President is even now, it is said, contemplating a withdrawal from the classified list of a very large number of persons, put thereon by the last administration. The outlook, therefore, for good civil service in the Philippines can scarcely be said to be good.

The islands may be held under a temporary military dictatorship during the period of preparation for statehood. There may have been in the past military despotisms which were mild and benign. If such there were the historian has not recounted them. They are of necessity arbitrary and by reason of the inherent weakness of humanity, stern, often unjust, cruel and greatly injurious both to the governors and the governed. They lead as surely as fate to that condition of things which now exists in Europe, namely, "where every peasant is born with a soldier on his back." They are reactionary and utterly opposed to the political philosophy of the age and destructive of the spirit of freedom.

In this connection I am assuming that this military occupation will be but temporary. It would be like that military control of the Indian which was designed to keep him in order until such time as he should die a natural death or be destroyed by the Indian agent sent from Washington. It cannot be denied that the military control of the Indian was good, but it was exactly the same kind of control which is exercised over convicts in a penitentiary, and it will scarcely be asserted that it was beneficial either to the Indian or the soldier. We must also assume that "Philippine agents" will be quite as numerous; quite as intelligently selected and quite as devoted to the best interests of the Malay, the Chinee, the Mohammedan and the Negrito as his prototype has been to the Chippewa and the Sioux. And we have a similar right to assume that, armed with the same bibulous ammunition, he will as easily outstrip the school teacher and the evangelist as did his predecessor with the red man of the plains.

But it is said that this occupation will be but temporary and that as soon as the native is educated to the point of citizenship the colonies will be admitted to statehood. It may be that political parties are arrived at that millenium when they will, before adding to the number of stars on our flag, cautiously and wisely consider all the questions requisite to citizenship before this vital action is taken. It may be that the Democrat will cease to yearn for a majority in both Houses of Congress; that the Republican has reached that altitude of virtue at which he will refuse to avail himself of such golden opportunity for gaining party supremacy. If so, we have progressed greatly since the Dakotas, Montana, Wyoming and Idaho, with a population absurdly smaller than the Philippines, were admitted to the Union, for well known partisan purposes. It is a part of our history that States have been admitted just as soon as the dominant party in Congress could find a reasonable excuse for so doing, provided their admission would contribute to partisan success. Such being the case it is just as certain that this temporary military occupation will be short lived, and that we shall have in the halls of Congress senators and representatives from Luzon and Mindanao as we have from Montana and the Dakotas, and it is equally certain that this action will return to plague its authors as did the admission of those States, when our economic policy was threatened by the shock of financial repudiation. As Carl Schurz has shrewdly remarked, as soon as they demonstrate that they are unfit for self-rule we shall admit them into the Union to help govern us.

There remains but one other method by which this territory can be maintained, and that is as a permanent colonial possession to be governed by such civil system as may be devised for the administration of affairs. In this connection it must be remembered that history shows no instance of a tropical people who have demonstrated a capacity for maintaining an enduring form of Republican government. That old patriot Simon Bolivar said, "Permanent republics can no more be maintained in the tropics than permanent furrows can be drawn in the sea." It must also be remembered that these people have within the last one hundred years initiated no less than twelve separate revolutions against the government of Spain. It is true the government of Spain was bad, but it was a military government and as such necessarily implies the use of force to subject the will of the many to the will and purposes of the few. The best military government on earth can do no less than this. Our Declaration of Independence says "We hold these truths to be self-evident, that all men are created equal, that they are endowed by their Creator with certain inalienable rights; that among these are life, liberty and the pursuit of happiness; that to secure those rights governments are instituted among men deriving their just powers from the consent of government." Unless these principles which are the basis of that constitution (which Gladstone said was the greatest instantaneous governmental charter ever created) are to be considered as a "nursery rhyme" or "swaddling clothes," it is still the vital principle upon which we must shape our national polity. It needs no argument to show that military despotism, however wisely administered, however free from those vicious qualities which usually inhere therein, can never be a government which derives its just powers from the consent of the governed; and if we, the people of the United States, who have never yet repudiated the doctrine contained in the preamble of our constitution which we ordained and established "in order to secure the blessings of liberty to ourselves and our posterity" are now prepared to say "Yes, we will still retain the blessings of liberty in the United States; we expended unlimited blood and treasure to abolish the wrong of human slavery in this country; but we will deliberately ordain and establish in our Philippine colony a different system, a system of human slavery, infinitely worse than that which we have here suppressed," then there is no extravagance in the prediction that our Republic is in its decadence. For the slavery of the African race in this country was more injurious to the master than the slave. His condition was never worse than that of a domestic animal and, bad as that was, the condition of the Filipino, the untamed and untamable, the uncivilizable Oriental, the man of superstition, of fanatism, incapable of such training as to render him useful, will be infinitely worse and he will surely follow in the footsteps of the Red Indian to extermination, the assured fate of every servient race. Picture then this desecration of our political idols ; we, the only people in history who have ever successfully maintained a free government, founded upon contract, the basis of which was the principle of liberty ; we, in the twinkling of an eye, throw down these ancient monuments, wrest from a conquered and helpless foe a territory which we do not need, at a price fixed by ourselves, for the purpose of enslaving its inhabitants and dragging in the dust of dishonor that emblem of freedom which it has been our boast for more than a hundred years to maintain in dignity and pride.

Assuming that we can establish a civil system either temporary or permanent, let us look into some of the probable workings thereof. Civil administration in our own country is not a thing in which we have a right to take much pride. In national affairs government by party has developed the fact that we can expend more public funds, for the purpose of maintaining party machinery, either in the form of pensions or salaries than any other nation on earth. Our success in this direction would bring the blush even to the cheek of a Walpole. Our municipal governments are failures so monumental that they would be ludicrous were not the consequences so terrible. Such national scandals as the Credit Mobilier and such municipal disgraces as are constantly to be seen in St. Louis and other large cities are a sufficient justification to assume that government by our civil system in the Philippines would at least be no better than our own. It is not overstating the case then, to say that on this assumption it is very questionable if such a system in the Philippines would be an improvement over the Spanish rule. The bribery and official corruption which have characterized that have, it is true, been open and unblushing, while with us it is carefully concealed under the form of law. But is ours any better for that reason?

But even after our system was created consider for a moment its administration.

Changes would of course take place with each change of political parties in this country. These changes would simply serve to admit a few more greedy politicians to the troughs vacated by their predecessors. Colonies 12,000 miles away are less liable to the troublesome visits of investigating committees than if within the confines of our country. It goes without saying that official malfeasance would be increased by imagined security from discovery. It will not do to say that Russia, England, France and Belgium have successfully maintained colonial possessions and therefore that we are able to do so. It must be remembered that these governments exist at home under monarchial systems. Colonial affairs are regulated either by the ukase of a sovereign or by orders in council. In a word, as Gladstone said, instead of being like our own based upon a theory of equality they are based on a theory of inequality. This implies the domination of one race over the other, one part of the people over another part of the people. It accounts for the success of monarchies in managing their colonies and it demonstrates the impossibility of our maintaining a colonial system consistent with the fundamental principles of our government. It must be remembered in this connection that the whole power of civil government of territory that we may acquire, no matter under what form it may be held, rests in Congress. The President cannot control it unless it be a purely military occupation. So that there can be no provision relating to the government of the Philippines save what is enacted by Congress as a law. Those who are familiar with Congressional methods and who know that the most meritorious bills are crowded out by political pressure, that the mass of legislation in each Congress is so great that continuous sessions day and night, year after year, without intermission, would not serve to consider one-half of them, will see how difficult, if not impossible, it would be to obtain needed legislation.

Again, if we are to adopt a colonial policy we must accept one of its inevitable consequences, that is to say, war. The isolation which has been ours since we became a nation has been our greatest protection. Until the Spanish war we have fought none save in self-defense or to settle the fundamental principles of our national existence ; but by taking colonial possessions we throw down the gauntlet into the arena of international strife. England, the greatest colonizer in Europe, has not been, during the long reign of Queen Victoria, for any two consecutive years, without a war. Aside from the cost and hideous concomitants of war itself let us not lose sight of the brutalizing and deteriorating effects of all save wars of patriotism, upon the people themselves. The English people to-day, good and great a people as they are; are nevertheless affected by the idea that commercial supremacy at the cost of war is not too dear. The history of that great nation is blotted on every page by instances of the deliberate institution of war for the purpose of acquiring territory.

Are we then to enroll ourselves amongst those who subscribe to this belief? Are we to be deceived by the glittering sophistry of those who hold that it is better to be a nation of warriors than a nation of shopkeepers? That by war we escape the menace and peril of socialism and agrarianism? Has not this very policy been the ruin of the French Republic, which is even now tottering to its fall and a return to Bourbonism? Does not the fact that England governs all her colonies to-day, except Canada and Australia, by pure military despotism without the consent of the governed, and taxes them without representation, serve to warn us? And what is the condition of her subject races in India? Admirable as is her civil system, after one hundred years' experience Lord Elgin, one of her famous Viceroys, said: "There is more of a bond between man and dog than there is between an Englishman and a Hindoo."

Our revolutionary war was not, it is true, begun by us with the idea of terminating the colonial system; for a year after it began our forefathers still called themselves British subjects. But is it not a fact that the final purpose and effect of that war was a rebellion against that system, meaning of course that system by which one country holds another in vassalage, governs it without the consent of the governed, and taxes it without representation? Are we now, we who have in the harbor of our greatest seaport the statue of "Liberty enlightening the world," are we to carry into the Orient the spirit which animated Alaric, the Goth, and Julius Cæser?

There is another serious problem which is likely to vex us in the management of this new acquisition. Nearly all the Europeans and those natives who have any religion whatever (other than the worshippers of the moon to whom allusion has been made), are Roman Catholics. Whatever system we devise, either under a civil or military occupation, must include some plan of education. Necessarily, if our own institutions are an analogue, this plan would be a secular one; and we shall then be confronted by the same paradox which confronted England in maintaining an established Episcopal Church in Ireland where four-fifths of the population were Roman Catholics. The cost of these schools must of course be paid by taxation. It is said that four-fifths of the lands which are of any value in the islands are owned by the Roman Catholic Church. Would it not be an awkward thing to have a plan of education, paid for by taxes upon the property of one religious sect for the secular education of the minority?

Is it not monstrous that we should at this time contemplate the establishment of an abuse which England has so recently remedied?

Another serious consideration presents itself the aspect of which is legal. Our national government has heretofore been able, as in the case of the mob violence against the Italians in New Orleans and the killing of Austrian subjects by the sheriff in the Latimer riots in Pennsylvania, to avoid making redress to those countries by shifting the responsibility upon state governments. Whether we establish a military dictatorship or a civil system in the Philippines (until we can confer statehood) foreign countries will hold the United States liable for any damage to citizens on that territory. And if we consider the character of the population, the remoteness from the centre of government, the cheapness of life amongst Orientals and their characteristic indifference to rights of property, this menace is of no small measure.

Then there is our tariff law. There is no question of the power of congress to impose different tariffs upon different parts of the country, (other than the states) but in the case of the Philippines we shall be confronted with this proposition : If we do not impose a protective tariff upon goods there imported, we admit the whole world to compete with our own manufacturers in one part of our own country. If we do impose a tariff upon imports there we are taxing them without their consent even upon the necessities of life. We will by this latter measure, by imposing a tariff against ourselves, do away with all the commercial benefits which it is desired we shall have. And if we do not impose a tariff against foreigners we stand no better chance than we now do to retain what trade we have or to secure more. And then unless we create the anomaly of maintaining our own protective tariff upon importations from the Philippines, a part of our own territory, we put our own farmers and manufacturers in competition with the pauper labor of the Orient, that bugbear of politicians. The sugar, tobacco and hemp growers of the Philippines who are willing to labor at about five cents a day will compete with the farmers of our southern and some of our northern states.

Amongst the industrial questions that present themselves is that of labor. No matter in what form we maintain the Philippines we must admit the inhabitants of that country into the United States if they wish to come here. We now have federal laws which prohibit the importation of foreign labor under contract and laws for the exclusion of the Chinese; but these laws would not operate (unless we simply intend to establish militarism in the Philippines and govern them as Russia governs her dependencies,) to exclude the Malay, the Chinee, the Mohammadan and even those worshippers of the moon, should they desire to come to the United States. Even Gov. Tanner could not exclude them from Illinois. These people with the exception of the last named, who do not work at all, are in the habit of working for from twenty to fifty cents a day. It is no demagogic appeal to the laboring classes to submit for their consideration this very serious aspect of the question.

The race question is perhaps the most serious of all problems arising in this connection. We are constantly deporting Chinese under the exclusion act and yet we are now on the eve of incorporating into our national body hundreds of thousands of Chinese Coolies; not the better class but the half castes, the dregs of China; more than one hundred thousand Mohammedans, thousands of savages and half-breeds of almost every kind and description—all Orientals. Are we forgetful of the fact that the racial differences between the Oriental and western races are never to be eradicated? The Oriental is of the past; he has not progressed for centuries; he hates progress. The constitution of China it is said has not been changed for thousands of years. We are progressive, energetic and intolerant of the very thing which is his most marked characteristic—indolence. The two races could never amalgamate. It is the part of wisdom for us who have not yet finished robbing and killing the aboriginal Indian and who are still unsuccessfully wrestling with the race question in the South; who have within the last three months fought an Indian war in Minnesota and a race war with negroes in Carolina, for a moment to contemplate the consequences of taking into our body politic millions of people—ignorant of and hostile to our laws, our language, our religion and the basic principle of our government?

We are not a nation who hesitate to incur an expense when it is our duty to do so. Yet is it not worth considering that the military occupation of these colonies on the basis of General Miles' estimate of 75,000 men and a squadron of twenty warships, would increase the national burden of taxation from its present very low rate, about five dollars per capita, upon production, to the rates prevalent in European countries of from eight to forty dollars per capita. This is what Edward Atkinson calls a state of passive war, a condition almost as wasteful and demoralizing as an active campaign. Has anyone yet pointed out how our eighty millions of people who are thus to be taxed are to receive an adequate return for the burdens which this will involve?

It is sometimes said that we in common with other European nations are the trustees of civilization in the tropics. It is a brilliant but deceptive aphorism.

It was not talked of in this connection until needed as an excuse for the freely predicted annexation of Cuba and the taking of the Philippines with the strong hand. Assuming it to mean that we are to aid in the establishment of civilization in the tropics, does not the higher civilization imply freedom and are we promoting this by our government by Major Generals in Puerto Rico and the Philippines? If we annex Cuba, even with the consent of those who have sufficient intelligence to give it, shall we not be the laughing stock of the world as having acquired a valuable property under false pretenses? And how grotesque is our attitude when we consider that this war to relieve the starving insurgents in Cuba has ended in being a war against the Philippines struggling for freedom from the tyranny of the same power? How can we render an account of our trust in the light of this singular situation?

We are told that these great national movements, such as the expansion idea are never favored by the intelligent classes; that they are the blind instincts of the masses of the people and that therefore they are nearly always right. If this is so history must be re-written. Great policies and great revolutions are not the creations of impulse, but of mind. The immediate cause of a revolution may be the revolt of the masses, but the forces which suggest and accomplish the ends in all such cases are the forces of intellect. If there be no better ground for the acquisition of the Philippines than the impulse of those who confessedly do not know the facts, and can give no reason, then the day of statesmen and publicists is at an end, and Jack Cades and Wat Tylers, not Gladstones and Washingtons, should control the affairs of men.

The records of the British Army in India show that out of seventy-five thousand men, thirteen thousand are each year sent back to England incapacitated by disease peculiar to the tropics and to tropical social conditions. No sacrifice of life is too great where a great principle is involved, but has it been shown that life is so cheap that we can barter it at such ruinous rates for commercial gain?

The unacknowledged cause for much of the sentiment for expansion is the zeal of the churches for the evangelization of the people of the Philippines. The purpose is commendable, of course, but its advocates mistake the function of government when they assume that conquest should be made for the extension of christianity. It is the old idea of sending out the missionary with a bible in one hand and a sword in the other. Is it not more becoming to an enlightened Christian people, that their missionaries should go forth with the bible in *both* hands? Can the most zealous evangelist maintain the proposition that it is well that many heathen should be put to the sword in order that some may be saved?

If it be urged that there are precedents for the proposed inclusion of the Philippine territory, the answer is easily found. Florida, Texas, Hawaii, the Louisiana Purchase and Alaska were acquired by contract : the Mexican cession, as a protection to and for the symmetrical development of our own country. In every case except Hawaii and Alaska either intrinsic value, obvious natural advantages, an unobjectionable population or contiguity have furnished ample justification. For Alaska and Hawaii no valid excuse can be given ; but partisan measures, leading up to national mistakes, can never suffice as authority for future policies.

Finally if we can eliminate sentimentalism, impulse and fictions as to trusteeship ; if we can divest our minds of the false idea that it is the business of constitutional governments to engage in national charities and to evangelize all the people of the earth ; if we can persuade ourselves to withhold our hand from the tinseled bauble of being a "world power," is it not wise to do so and to soberly take counsel together before we violate the traditions of a hundred years, change our form of government and align ourselves in action and policy with those monarchies which we have resolutely said shall not plant their feet upon American soil? Or shall we hold for naught the wisdom of the builders of our nation and at the bidding of a blind impulse bring to life that hybrid political monstrosity, that intolerable union of bondage and freedom, an Imperialistic Republic? Better "United States of America Limited," as some have sarcastically suggested, than "United States of America and Slave Colonies in Polynesia."

Printed by Libri Plureos GmbH in Hamburg, Germany